super simple
pressed flower projects

FUN AND EASY CRAFTS INSPIRED BY NATURE

Kelly Doudna

Consulting Editor, Diane Craig, M.A./Reading Specialist

A Division of ABDO

ABDO
Publishing Company

visit us at www.abdopublishing.com

Published by ABDO Publishing Company, a division of ABDO, P.O. Box 398166, Minneapolis, Minnesota 55439.
Copyright © 2014 by Abdo Consulting Group, Inc. International copyrights reserved in all countries. No part of this book may be reproduced in any form without written permission from the publisher. Super SandCastle™ is a trademark and logo of ABDO Publishing Company.

Printed in the United States of America, North Mankato, Minnesota
102013
012014

 PRINTED ON RECYCLED PAPER

Editor: Liz Salzmann
Content Developer: Nancy Tuminelly
Cover and Interior Design and Production: Kelly Doudna, Mighty Media, Inc.
Photo Credits: Kelly Doudna, Shutterstock

The following manufacturers/names appearing in this book are trademarks: Aleene's® Tacky Glue®, Darice® Jewelry Designer™, Elmer's®, Kittrich®, Mod Podge®

Library of Congress Cataloging-in-Publication Data
Doudna, Kelly, 1963-
  Super simple pressed flower projects : fun and easy crafts inspired by nature / Kelly Doudna ; consulting editor, Diane Craig, M.A./reading specialist.
    pages cm. -- (Super simple nature crafts)
  Audience: Age 5-10.
  ISBN 978-1-62403-081-9
1. Handicraft--Juvenile literature. 2. Nature craft--Juvenile literature. 3. Flowers--Juvenile literature. I. Title.
  TT157.D638 2014
  745.594--dc23
                        2013022901

Super SandCastle™ books are created by a team of professional educators, reading specialists, and content developers around five essential components—phonemic awareness, phonics, vocabulary, text comprehension, and fluency—to assist young readers as they develop reading skills and strategies and increase their general knowledge. All books are written, reviewed, and leveled for guided reading, early reading intervention, and Accelerated Reader® programs for use in shared, guided, and independent reading and writing activities to support a balanced approach to literacy instruction.

to adult Helpers

The craft projects in this series are fun and simple. There are just a few things to remember to keep kids safe. Some projects require the use of sharp or hot objects. Also, kids may be using messy materials such as glue or paint. Make sure they protect their clothes and work surfaces. Review the projects before starting, and be ready to assist when necessary.

Key Symbol

Look for this warning symbol in this book.

SHARP!
You will be working with a sharp object. Get help!

contents

fabulous flowers

We love to smell flowers. We love having a vase of flowers on the table. But a flower is more than just a pretty face! The art of pressing flowers is a great way to save beautiful blooms.

And once flowers have been pressed, you can get creative. Try the fun and simple projects in this book. Nature made the flowers. You can make the crafts!

hydrangea

pansies

sunflower

4

CHOOSing flowers

The best flowers to press are flat and have one layer of **petals**. Good choices are pansies, violets, and impatiens. You can also press the individual **florets** from flowers such as geraniums and hydrangeas. For round flowers such as roses, carefully cut the flower head in half. Then press each half separately. Flowers such as coneflowers and sunflowers have thick centers. They won't press well. But you can pull off their petals and press those.

Pick flowers after dew and raindrops have dried. Take a basket with you. Flowers will last longer if you handle them less. Put them in your flower press as soon as you can. If you can't do that right away, put the flowers in the refrigerator to keep them fresh.

safety tip
When you are picking flowers, watch out for thorns and stinging insects such as bees.

FLOWERS in tHiS BOOK

These are some of the flowers we pressed for the projects in this book.

bachelor button

aster

lobilia

cosmos

begonia

hosta

impatiens

star flower

marigold

Russian sage

petunia

geranium

phlox

wildflowers

Pro tip

Flower presses press harder in the middle than at the edges. Put thicker flowers in the middle. Place thin flowers near the edges.

fun tip

Don't just press whole flowers. Press leaves and single **petals** too. You can use them in **designs**. Or you can get creative and make **butterflies** and other creatures.

Pro tip

Plan your project. Draw your design on paper. Lay out the flowers in different ways. Find an arrangement you like. Then put the project together.

7

WHat YOU'LL NEED

Here are many of the things you will need to do the projects in this book. You can find some of them around the house or yard. You can get others at a craft store or hardware store.

pressed flowers

carriage bolts

wing nuts

washers

boards

corrugated cardboard

paper

polyester batting

fabric

ribbon

votive candle holders

spray glue

Mod Podge

craft glue

light switch plate

lamp shade

CD

tweezers

clear contact paper

metal hoop

suction cup window hanger

clear packing tape

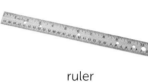

ruler

foam brush

earring findings

elastic jewelry cord

scissors

screwdriver

pencil

hole punch

small craft hole punch

needle-nose pliers

tissue paper

make a flower press

Decorate your flower press with some of the flowers that you press.

WHAT YOU'LL NEED

4 carriage bolts, 4" × ¼" × 20

4 wing nuts, ¼" × 20

8 washers, ¼"

2 boards, 8 × 12 inches, with aligned ¼" holes drilled in the corners

scissors

6 pieces of corrugated cardboard, 8 × 12 inches, with the corners cut off

6 pieces of plain paper, 8½ × 11 inches, with the corners cut off

tweezers

3 pieces of ½-inch-thick polyester batting, 8 × 12 inches, with the corners cut off

2 pieces of fabric, 8 × 12 inches, with the corners cut off

spray glue

1. Put a washer onto each carriage bolt. Put a bolt through each of the holes in one board.

2. Lay the board on a flat surface. The bolts should be sticking up. Add layers of flowers to be pressed. Use one of the methods on the next two pages.

3. Place the second board on top. The bolts should go through the corner holes.

4. Put a washer onto each carriage bolt. Screw a wing nut onto each bolt. Tighten the wing nuts. This presses the layers together.

5. Let your press sit for two weeks. Remove the wing nuts. Remove the top board. Carefully use tweezers to remove the pressed flowers. Now the flowers are ready to use!

PRO tiP

Make a mark on each board. Then it will be easy to line up the holes.

Simple Pressing

1 Place a piece of cardboard on the bottom board. Lay a piece of paper on the cardboard.

2 Lay flowers on the paper. Do not **overlap** the flowers. Cover them with another piece of paper. Top with another piece of cardboard.

3 Repeat layers if you have more flowers. Make up to three layers of flowers.

 Pro tip

Keep track of what's on each layer. Write flower names on sticky notes. Put the notes on the edges of the layers.

 Pro tip

After two weeks, loosen the wing nuts. Leave the flowers in the press for two more days. This will make them easier to remove.

Padded Pressing

Make padded boards for more even pressing. Use a board with one layer of batting for flat flowers such as pansies. Use a board with two layers of batting for thicker flowers such as sunflowers.

1. To make a thin padded board spray one side of a piece of cardboard with glue. Lay a piece of batting on the cardboard.

2. Spray glue on top of the batting. Lay a piece of fabric on the batting. Press the layers together firmly.

3. To make a thick padded board repeat steps 1 and 2. Use two layers of batting instead of one.

4. Use one of your padded boards in place of the bottom piece of cardboard. The padded side should face up. Then add a layer of flowers. Cover the flowers with a piece of paper. Put a piece of cardboard on top.

BOOKMARKS

These beautiful bookmarks will make any book better.

WHAT YOU'LL NEED

clear contact paper

scissors

pressed flowers

tweezers

ruler

hole punch

ribbon

1. Cut two sheets of contact paper. They should be the same size. Peel the backing off one sheet. Lay it down with the sticky side up.

2. Lay the flowers on the contact paper. Arrange them in narrow rows. Leave at least ½ inch (1.3 cm) between rows.

3. Peel the backing off the other sheet of contact paper. Lay it over the flowers with the sticky side down. Rub firmly to seal the flowers in.

4. Cut between the rows to make bookmarks. You can cut straight edges or follow the shape of the flowers. Trim any sticky edges.

5. Punch a hole in the top of each bookmark. Thread a piece of ribbon through the hole. Tie a knot close to the edge of the bookmark.

get fancy

Use a narrow piece of colored tissue paper as a background for the flowers.

CANDLE HOLDERS

Brighten the room with a gorgeous glow.

WHAT YOU'LL NEED

scissors

tissue paper (plain or colored)

clear glass votive candle holders

foam brush

Mod Podge

pressed flowers

1 Cut a strip of tissue paper long enough to wrap around the candle holder.

2 Coat the outside of the candle holder with Mod Podge. Press the tissue paper onto the holder.

3 Brush another coat of Mod Podge over the tissue paper. Add pressed flowers. Let it dry.

4 Brush a top coat of Mod Podge over everything. Let it dry.

 variation

Make a pretty pencil holder. Use a clear drinking glass instead of a candle holder.

 get fancy

Use more than one color of tissue paper.

switch plate

A light switch cover festooned with flowers adds a touch of fancy to any room.

WHAT YOU'LL NEED

foam brush

Mod Podge

smooth light switch plate

pressed flowers

tweezers

screwdriver

1 Coat the switch plate with Mod Podge.

2 Use a tweezers to arrange pressed flowers on the switch plate. Press them down firmly. Let it dry.

3 Brush on a top coat of Mod Podge. Let it dry.

4 Screw the switch plate to the wall. Use the screws to poke through anything covering the screw holes. Tighten with the screwdriver.

 **Pro tip**

Trim anything hanging over the edges of the switch plate.

mandala

A marvelous mandala seems magical.

WHAT YOU'LL NEED

paper
pencil
old CD
pressed flowers
tweezers
foam brush
Mod Podge
scissors
ruler
ribbon

1. Plan your mandala. Trace around the CD on a piece of paper. Lay out some pressed flowers. Create a **design** you like.

2. Coat the plain side of the CD with Mod Podge. Add the pressed flowers. Leave the center hole open. Let it dry.

3. Brush on a thin top coat of Mod Podge. Let it dry.

4. Cut a 12-inch (30 cm) piece of ribbon. Put it through the center hole of the CD. Tie the ends together. Hang your mandala.

 Pro tip

When you apply Mod Podge, brush from the center of the CD to the edge. This will add to the design of your mandala.

 fun fact

A mandala represents the universe. People in different parts of the world make different types of mandalas. Most mandalas have a pattern of colorful circles and squares.

LAMP SHADE

Liven up the living room with a lovely lamp shade.

WHAT YOU'LL NEED

foam brush

Mod Podge

lamp shade (paper works best)

pressed flowers

ribbon

scissors

craft glue

1 Brush Mod Podge on the areas of the shade where you want to place the flowers. Add the flowers. Let it dry.

2 Carefully brush a top coat of Mod Podge over the flowers. Let it dry.

3 Cut a piece of ribbon a little longer than the bottom edge of the shade. Glue it on.

 Pro tip

Use a dab of craft glue on the back of larger or thicker flowers. This will help them stick to the shade better.

 Pro tip

You will be able to see the Mod Podge on the shade even after it dries. Brush it on carefully. Try to have as little extra around the edges of the flowers as possible.

sun catcher

Hang up this circle of color for a burst of brightness.

24

1. Plan your sun catcher. Trace around the metal hoop on a piece of paper. Lay out some pressed flowers. Create a **design** you like.

2. Trace the hoop two times on the backing of the contact paper. Trace it once on the tissue paper.

3. Cut out each circle. Cut outside the lines on the contact paper. Leave about ½ inch (1.3 cm) extra. Cut the tissue paper on the line.

continued on the next page

Pro tip

There will be space between the two layers of contact paper. That makes this project a good one for thicker pressed flowers.

25

4 Put a few small dots of glue around the edge of the tissue paper circle. Lay the metal hoop on the circle.

5 Peel the backing off one contact paper circle. Lay your pressed flowers on the sticky side. The fronts of the flowers should face down.

6 Lay the hoop and tissue paper over the flowers. The hoop should face down.

7 Roll the edge of the contact paper over the hoop. Press firmly.

8 Peel the backing off the second contact paper circle. Lay the hoop and flowers on the sticky side. The flowers should face up. Roll the edge of the contact paper over the hoop. Press firmly.

9 Poke a hole through all layers of the sun catcher at the top. Thread a piece of ribbon through the hole. Tie the ends to make a **loop**.

10 Stick the suction cup hanger on a window. Hang up your sun catcher.

✳ get fancy

Glue a piece of matching ribbon around the outside of the hoop.

jewelry

Make whimsical wearables with beautiful blooms.

WHAT YOU'LL NEED

pressed flowers

clear packing tape

scissors

small craft hole punch

2 earring findings

needle-nose pliers

ruler

elastic jewelry cord

Prepare the Flowers

1 Choose two pressed flowers for earrings. They should be the same kind and size.

2 Choose four or five flowers for a **bracelet**. They can all be the same. Or they can be different.

3 Lay the flowers on the sticky side of a piece of packing tape. Cover with more packing tape. Firmly press the pieces of tape together. This seals in the flowers.

Earrings

1 Cut out the earring flowers. Cut close to their edges. Don't cut so close that you break the seal. Leave a small tab of tape sticking out.

2 Punch a hole in the tab on each flower.

3 Put an earring finding through the hole in each flower.

Bracelet

1 Cut out the **bracelet** flowers. Cut close to their edges. Don't cut so close that you break the seal. Leave a small tab of tape sticking out from each side of each flower.

2 Punch two holes in each tab.

3 Wrap the elastic cord long around your wrist. Add 2 inches (5 cm). Cut two pieces that length.

4 Put a cord through a flower tab hole. Thread it through a tab hole on the other side of the flower. Thread the cord through the other flowers the same way. Thread the second cord through the remaining holes.

5 Tie the ends of the cords together. Trim any extra cord close to the knot.

✳ **get fancy**
Use metallic elastic cord to make your bracelet **sparkle**.

conclusion

Aren't pressed flowers great? You have let the beauty of nature come through with these wonderful pressed flower crafts. If you had fun, don't stop here. How else can you use pressed flowers?

And check out the other books in the Super Simple Nature Crafts series. You'll find projects that use ice, leaves, pinecones, seashells, and twigs. The ideas are endless!

glossary

bracelet – a pretty band or chain worn around the wrist.

butterfly – a thin insect with large brightly colored wings.

design – a decorative pattern or arrangement.

festooned – decorated.

floret – a small flower, especially one that is part of a bigger flower.

loop – a circle made by a rope, string, or thread.

overlap – to make something lie partly on top of something else.

petal – one of the thin, colored parts of a flower.

sparkle – to shine with flashes of light.